How to Implement and Supervise a Learning Style Program

Rita Dunn

Association for Supervision and Curriculum Development
Alexandria, Virginia

Association for Supervision and Curriculum Development
1250 N. Pitt Street • Alexandria, Virginia 22314
Telephone: (703) 549-9110 • Fax: (703) 299-8631

Gene R. Carter, *Executive Director*
Michelle Terry, *Assistant Executive Director, Program Development*
Ronald S. Brandt, *Assistant Executive Director*
Nancy Modrak, *Managing Editor, ASCD Books*
Darcie Simpson, *Associate Editor*
Mary Riendeau, *Project Assistant*
Gary Bloom, *Manager, Design and Production Services*
Tracey A. Smith, *Print Production Coordinator*
Cynthia Stock, *Desktop Publisher*

Printed in the United States of America.
ASCD Stock No. 196010
s4/96
$8.95

Library of Congress Cataloging-in-Publication Data
Dunn, Rita Stafford, 1930–
     How to implement and supervise a learning style program / Rita
Dunn.
        p. cm.
     Includes bibliographical references (p.   ).
     ISBN 0-87120-259-X
     1. Learning. 2. Cognitive styles—United States. 3. School
supervision—United States. I. Title.
     LB1060.D86 1996
     370.15'23—dc20   96-9955
                                                                CIP

00 99 98 97 96   5 4 3 2 1

How to Implement and Supervise a Learning Style Program

About The Author

Rita Dunn is a Professor at St. John's University's Division of Administrative and Instructional Leadership, and Director of St. John's University's Center for the Study of Learning and Teaching Styles, School of Education and Human Services, 8000 Utopia Parkway, Jamaica, NY 11439. Phone: (718) 990-6335.

Acknowledgments

The following learning style staff developers graciously shared with me the expertise they developed as they introduced and implemented style-responsive strategies in schools and districts throughout the United States and the world. I sincerely appreciate the anecdotes and guidelines they shared with me.

Duane Alm, Principal, C.C. Lee Elementary School, Aberdeen, S.D.

Peter Barrans, Vice Principal, Francis Liebermann Catholic High School, Scarborough, Ontario, Canada

Carolyn Brunner, Coordinator, Erie 1 BOCES International Learning Styles Center, Cheektowaga, N.Y.

Penny Claudis, Learning Styles Coordinator, Caddo Schools, Shreveport, La.

Ray Cooley, Principal, Junior High School #93, Buffalo, N.Y.

Wanda Dean, Principal, Oxford Elementary School, Oxford, Miss.

Thomas C. DeBello, Principal, Setauket Elementary School, East Setauket, N.Y.

Joan DellaValle, Principal, Otsego Elementary School, Dix Hills, N.Y.

Sherrye Dotson, District Curriculum Coordinator, Jacksonville Public Schools, Jacksonville, Texas

Mary Fisher, Principal, City Elementary School, Winner, S.D.

Larry Howie, Teacher, John A. McManus Elementary School, Chico, Calif.

Bart Kelliher, Director of Special Education and Special Services, The Buffalo City Schools, Buffalo, N.Y.

Dorothy Logan-Alexander, Assistant Superintendent, Brookhaven School District, Brookhaven, Miss.

Mary Laffey, Principal, Oakland Junior High School, Columbia, Miss.

Sister Natalie Lafser, Director, Office of Learning Styles, Saint Louis Archdiocese, St. Louis, Mo.

Jan Meritt, Science Teacher, Klammath Union High School, Klammath Falls, Ore.

Nancy Murphree, Mathematics Department Chair, Jacksonville Middle School, Jacksonville, Texas

Denise Parker, Developmental Reading Teacher, Oakland Junior High School, Columbia, Mo.

Richard Quinn, Superintendent, The Buffalo City Schools, Buffalo, N.Y.

Denise Stephenson, English Teacher, East Davidson High School, Thomasville, N.C.

Jody Sands Taylor, Adjunct Professor, University of Virginia, Richmond, Va.

Mary E. White, Mathematics Teacher, Oak Martin Middle School, Birmingham, Ala.

Regina White, Principal, Bulkley Middle School, Rhinebeck, N.Y.

1
All About Learning Styles

MANY PEOPLE PREFER TO LEARN IN WAYS THAT ARE DIFFERENT FROM how other people of the same class, grade, age, nationality, race, culture, or religion prefer to learn. How people prefer to learn is their *learning style preference.*

Although some gifted students can learn proficiently without using their learning style preferences, low achievers perform significantly better when they capitalize on their preferences. A decade of research demonstrates that both low and average achievers earn higher scores on standardized achievement tests and attitude tests when taught through their learning style preferences (Dunn, Griggs, Olson, Gorman, and Beasley 1995).

How Do Learning Styles Develop?

More than three-fifths of a person's learning style is biologically imposed (Restak 1979, Thies 1979). While concentrating on new and difficult academic information, an individual's learning style preferences include

- Quiet or background noise
- Bright or low light
- Formal or casual seating
- Uninterrupted study or intermittent breaks
- Perceptual modes (auditory, visual, tactile, and kinesthetic)
- No intake or intake (snacking, chewing, drinking, or smoking)
- Specific periods during the day

- Passivity or mobility
- Global or analytic processing styles

Even among family members, learning styles vary. Mothers and fathers tend to have diametrically opposite learning styles, children often reflect the partial style of one parent but not the other, siblings learn differently from each other, and offspring do not necessarily reflect either parent's style (Dunn and Griggs 1990, 1995; Milgram, Dunn, and Price 1993). Because of the differences between their styles, one sibling may perform well while another may perform inadequately or unevenly in traditional schools, which primarily respond to the styles of motivated, conforming, analytic learners. The siblings also relate differently to their parents.

Other elements develop as an outgrowth of students' experiences. Developmental elements of learning styles include

- Motivation
- A need for less or more structure
- Conformity versus nonconformity
- Sociological preferences for learning (Restak 1979, Thies 1979)

Preferences for learning styles change over time (Dunn and Griggs 1995). However, during a period in which an individual has strong style preferences, that person will achieve most easily when taught with strategies and resources that complement those preferences. Although many people can learn basic information through an incompatible style, even accomplished professionals learn most easily through their learning style strengths. The important thing to remember is that no single style is better or worse than any other (Dunn, Griggs, Olson, Gorman, and Beasley 1995). Everyone can learn; we just learn differently.

The Learning Styles of Gifted Students

Although all gifted students do not have the same learning style, they and their peers have learning styles that differ significantly from those of underachievers. Differences

2

in style also have been reported between the learning disabled and the gifted; between the learning disabled and average achievers; among different types of special education students; and among secondary students in comprehensive high schools and their counterparts in vocational education and industrial arts (St. John's University's Center for the Study of Learning and Teaching Styles 1996).

Adolescents gifted in a particular domain—athletics, dance, leadership, literature, mathematics, and music—revealed similar learning styles across nine cultures. The gifted in each intelligence area reported similar preferences for learning style—but those preferences were different from the preferences of other gifted groups and from the preferences of the nongifted (Milgram, Dunn, and Price 1993). The information that gifted adolescents in the same intelligence areas reveal almost identical learning styles across nine diverse cultures tends to corroborate Restak's (1979) and Thies' (1979) data that almost three-fifths of variables in the Dunn and Dunn Learning Style Models (1992, 1993) are biological.

Although gifted students prefer kinesthetic (experiential and active) and tactile (hands-on) instruction, many are able to learn auditorially and visually (Dunn 1989; Milgram, Dunn, and Price 1993). Low achieving students who also prefer kinesthetic and tactile learning, however, can *only* master difficult information through those modalities. In addition, low achievers often have only one or no perceptual strength in contrast with the multiperceptual strengths of the gifted (Dunn 1988; Dunn, Beaudry, and Klavas 1989; Kyriacou and Dunn 1994; Milgram, Dunn, and Price 1993).

Gifted adolescents in nine cultures preferred to learn either by themselves or with an authoritative teacher. If those students represent gifted students worldwide, cooperative learning and small-group instructional strategies should not be imposed on them. Few gifted and talented students want to learn with classmates. Even in the primary grades, gifted first- and second-graders revealed higher achievement and attitude test scores when learning in accordance with their sociological preferences (Perrin

1984). In just one year, 13 percent of those gifted young children completed between two and six years of grade-level curriculum in both rote memory and problem-solving tasks primarily by teaching themselves or occasionally working with other gifted classmates.

Although some gifted adolescents learn well early in the morning, many more prefer late morning, afternoon, or evening for concentrating on challenging academic studies (Milgram, Dunn, and Price 1993). Research documents the influence of time-of-day energy patterns on achievement (Andrews 1990; Dunn 1989; Dunn, Dunn, Primavera, Sinatra, and Virostko 1987; Lemmon 1985; Stone 1992). Conventional school hours appear to be poorly timed—for the majority of gifted adolescents *and* low achievers the best time for learning is other than early morning. Conventional school hours are appropriate for a minority of K–12 learners—no single period during the day is preferred by more than 40 percent of students. Before high school, the percentage for that preference is even lower. (Dunn and Dunn 1992, 1993; Milgram, Dunn, and Price 1993).

Of the gifted and talented we tested for hemispheric processing style, 19 percent were analytic, 26 percent were global, and 55 percent were integrated processors who functioned in either style when interested in the curriculum. Although both global and analytic students can be gifted, both textbooks and teachers' styles tend to be analytic. Conversely, emphasis on a thematic approach to curriculum (Dunn and Dunn 1972) is likely to work for global students but will then transfer the handicap to analytic students. Thus, until teachers instruct each group of processors

> *I implemented learning styles in my regular 11th grade English class. I used the identical curriculum in my traditionally taught accelerated 11th grade English class. My regular students outscored the accelerated students!*
>
> Denise Stephenson, Teacher, Thomasville, N.C.

differently, or students learn to teach themselves, conventional schooling will continue to benefit some and inhibit others.

The Learning Styles of Low Achievers

Seven learning style traits discriminate between high-risk students and dropouts, and students who perform well in school. Most low achievers and dropouts need

- Frequent opportunities for mobility
- Reasonable choices of how, with which resources, and with whom to learn
- A variety of instructional environments, materials, and sociological groupings rather than routines and patterns
- To learn during late morning, afternoon, or evening hours
- Informal seating (e.g., beanbag chairs and cushions)
- Soft illumination—bright or fluorescent light may contribute to hyperactivity
- Introduction to materials with tactile or visual resources, reinforced with visual or kinesthetic resources; or an introduction to materials with kinesthetic or visual resources, reinforced with visual or tactile resources

Underachievers tend to have poor auditory memory. If they learn visually, it usually is through pictures, drawings, graphs, symbols, comics, and cartoons rather than text. Although low achievers often want to do well in school, their inability to remember facts through lecture, discussion, or reading contributes to their low performance in traditional schools where introductory instruction is usually teachers talking and students listening or reading (Dunn 1988). Although low achievers learn differently from high achievers and the gifted, they also learn differently from each other.

How Does Culture Contribute to Achievement?

Research by Milgram, Dunn, and Price (1993) reveals that opportunity substantially influences an individual's development of specific talents. For example, if access to creative activities, information, or role models is not readily

> *Children in grades 3–12 have gone from* D*'s and* F*'s to* A*'s after using tactile and kinesthetic materials. Achievement scores keep rising. It's working, and we've seen improvement each year since 1988.*
>
> Sister Natalie Lafser, Director, St. Louis, Mo.

available, fewer adolescents will develop giftedness in that domain. Thus, in cultures that respect science, higher percentages of students gifted in science will develop. The same finding holds firm across other domains. Most U.S. communities support athletics financially, but rarely hesitate to eliminate programs in music, art, and drama when funds are scarce. In addition, few advanced science opportunities are available to elementary school and middle school students.

Why Emphasize Standardized Achievement Test Scores? When legislative groups, state education departments, boards of education, communities, and the media criticize the level of student literacy in the United States and demand increased accountability for standardized achievement test scores, we cannot continue to blame low achievement on everything except on how we teach. The significantly higher standardized achievement test scores of learning disabled and emotionally handicapped students in learning style schools suggest that this instructional approach may be the key for many poor achievers (Alberg, Cook, Fiore, Friend, Sano 1992; Andrews 1990; Brunner and Majewski 1990; Klavas 1993; Kyriacou and Dunn 1994, Quinn 1993, Stone 1992). After all, if students classified as special education cannot perform well on tests, how do we explain their improved test scores in learning style classrooms? Admittedly, many poor achievers do not function well under stress, but their stress appears sufficiently reduced after learning through their preferences to enable them to attain significantly higher scores on tests (Dunn, Griggs, Olson, Gorman, and Beasley 1995).

Better Ways to Assess Skills. Because students do have different learning styles and intelligences, when possible or appropriate they should be able to show how much they have learned by using their unique talents and interests. Thus, a musically gifted student should be allowed to explain a topic by singing; an artistic student should be able to draw or illustrate an explanation of a topic. These alternatives do not eliminate pencil-and-paper tests—they are additional ways for students to show how much they have learned.

One aspect of authentic assessment is a portfolio of accumulated projects and demonstrations of mastery. As an alternative to testing, portfolios are reasonable as long as educators and parents remember the following points:

- Underachievers who have been taught through their learning style strengths can and do demonstrate mastery on pencil and paper tests.
- Students need to learn to take standardized achievement tests or their chances for being accepted into institutions of higher learning and for receiving scholarships will be sharply reduced (Levy and Riordan 1995).
- The public will not believe that students who demonstrate content mastery through performance measures are as able as those who also make high scores on tests.
- Test-taking is a skill that all students need to and can master.
- Minority students and underachievers who perform least well on standardized achievement tests may suffer from being excused from taking them. These children will be viewed as incapable by some; eventually, they may perceive themselves as incapable. Fewer experiences taking tests will further diminish their ability to handle tests confidently. When children believe that they cannot perform well on tests, they do not.

Visitors to our learning style inclusion classes cannot tell the "special" students from the "regular" students.

Wanda Dean, Principal, Oxford, Miss.

Rather than eliminating testing, it seems sensible to require that teachers teach using learning styles and then give the students opportunities to demonstrate how well they learn. We should strive to transform all of our schools into learning style schools.

Authentic learning style schools are different from any other kind of school you have ever visited—and they don't cost a dollar more. Unlike traditional education, the open classrooms of the '60s and '70s, and the "brain-based" practices that some enthusiasts currently advocate, learning style schools acknowledge that children learn differently from each other. In learning style schools, teachers focus on teaching students how to (1) recognize and rely on their personal learning style strengths, (2) teach themselves and each other by using those strengths, and (3) learn the lesson by using the most appropriate resources and approaches.

Learning style schools offer a variety of instructional resources. Students may focus on identical information and skills while working in sections of the classroom that best meet their personal environmental, emotional, and physiological styles—and many will have made the materials they're using. Whole classes rarely engage in either teacher-directed instruction or cooperative learning groups. Instead, children learn on the basis of their individual sociological preferences—alone, with a classmate or two, in a small cooperative or competitive group, or with their teacher. Students may vary their choices, but are encouraged to use their strengths whenever the academic material is complex or difficult for them.

Practitioners in the United States report statistically higher standardized achievement test scores and grade point averages for students transferred from traditional classrooms to learning style classrooms at the elementary (Andrews 1990; Koshuta and Koshuta 1993; Lemmon 1985; Neely and Alm 1992, 1993; Quinn 1993; Stone 1992; Turner 1993), secondary (Brunner and Majewski 1990; Elliot 1991; Gadwa and Griggs 1985; Harp and Orsak 1990; Orsak 1990a, b; Perrin 1990; Quinn 1993), and college (Clark-Thayer 1987;

Lenehan, Dunn, Ingham, Murray, and Signer 1994; Mickler and Zippert 1987; Nelson, Dunn, Griggs, Primavera, and Fitzpatrick 1993) levels.

Improved achievement is often apparent after only six weeks of learning styles instruction. After one year, teachers report that their students earn much higher standardized achievement and attitude test scores than before.

> *We had an increase of 18 points on the math portion of our students' SATs in the first year we implemented learning styles!*
>
> Larry Howie, Teacher, Chico, Calif.

How to Identify Learning Styles

To accurately identify students' learning styles, teachers must have a reliable and valid instrument because some characteristics are not discernable, even to the experienced educator (Beaty 1986; Dunn, Dunn, and Price 1977; Marcus 1977). In addition, teachers may misinterpret students' behaviors and misunderstand the symptoms. For example, it is difficult to determine whether a youngster's hyperactivity is a need for mobility, variety, informal seating, kinesthetic resources, intermittent breaks, nonconformity, or discipline.

Instruments for identifying learning styles should do more than identify one or two variables on a bipolar continuum. A comprehensive instrument enhances the teacher's ability to prescribe instructional alternatives and the student's chance for significant academic improvement (Griggs, Griggs, Dunn, and Ingham 1994). Learning styles are a multidimensional construct; many variables affect each other and produce unique patterns. Those patterns suggest how each person is likely to concentrate, process, internalize, and retain new and difficult information, and which reading or math teaching strategies are most likely to be effective with a particular student (Dunn, Dunn, and Perrin 1994).

2
Taking the First Steps

RECOGNIZE THAT THE PRACTICE OF LEARNING STYLES HELPS STUDENTS achieve. At least 70 percent of students cannot remember three-quarters of what they either hear or read, and many of those do not read well. Such learners do not feel good about themselves in a classroom dominated by listening and reading. Therefore, it is important to identify students' learning styles to determine their perceptual strengths and to teach them how to capitalize on their strengths. Begin with a commitment to learning style approaches to help your students become academically successful and independent. Then decide how to assess your students and proceed with implementing learning style training.

Inventory Students' Learning Styles

One way to inventory students' styles is to develop styles-responsive resources, design a variety of classroom environments, and experiment with each slowly and diligently for each child. Your teachers will need to track the relative effectiveness of each resource for each child, and should be aware that even experienced teachers have difficulty in accurately identifying children's learning styles through observation (Beaty 1986, Marcus 1977). Of course, even if your teachers use an inventory, they will need to track each student's performance.

If your district has the resources, use one of the instruments on the market. A reliable and valid comprehensive instrument reveals which learners are affected by which elements of style. Only three comprehensive models exist for students in grades 3–12, and each has a related instrument designed to reveal individuals' styles based on the traits examined by that model (DeBello 1990). These models are *NASSP Learning Style Profile* (Keefe, Languis, Letteri, and Dunn 1986), *Cognitive Style Interest Inventory* (Hill 1976), and the *Learning Style Inventory* (*LSI*) (Dunn, Dunn, and Price 1989). The *LSI* is the most reliable of these three instruments, and has been periodically revised since 1974. The reliability and validity of the *LSI* were confirmed in the '70s by researchers at the National Center for Research in Vocational Education at Ohio State University (Kirby 1979), and more recently by other research (Dunn, DellaValle, Dunn, Geisert, Sinatra, and Zenhausern 1986; Dunn, Giannitti, Murray, Geisert, Rossi, and Quinn 1990; Dunn, Griggs, Olson, Gorman, and Beasley 1995; Dunn, Krimsky, Murray, and Quinn 1985; Lenehan, Dunn, Ingham, Murray, and Signer 1994).

Don't administer the LSI *until you have training and realistic expectations. It takes three to five years for the staff to embrace the philosophy and to develop real learning style classrooms.*

June Hodgin, Teacher and Learning Styles Consultant,
Abilene, Texas

What Does the *LSI* Do?

The *Learning Style Inventory* (Dunn, Dunn, and Price 1989) assesses an individual's preferences in the following areas: (a) physical environment (sound, light, temperature, and seating); (b) emotional stimuli (motivation, persistence, responsibility, conformity, and internal or external structure); (c) social needs (learning alone, in a pair, as part of a small group, with an authoritative or collegial adult, in a variety of ways, or in a consistent pattern); (d) physiological factors (perceptual modalities, food or liquid intake, time-of-day energy levels, mobility needs); and (e) cognitive processing inclinations—either global (right) or analytic (left) inclinations (Dunn, Bruno, Sklar, Zenhausern, and Beaudry 1990; Dunn, Cavanaugh, Eberle, and Zenhausern 1982). See Figure 2.1 on page 14.

The *Learning Style Inventory*

- Identifies how each student prefers to learn;
- Reports the consistency of each student's responses;
- Provides a summary of each student's preferred learning style;
- Describes the social environment in which each student is likely to achieve most effectively;
- Identifies the student's preference for variety or routine;
- Sequences the student's perceptual strengths, indicating which styles should be used to begin and to reinforce studies, and which to use for homework;
- Extrapolates information to determine if the student is a conformist or a nonconformist;
- Indicates if snacks are an integral part of the student's learning process;
- Notes if mobility may accelerate the student's learning process;
- Analyzes the student's answers for a consistency profile;
- Suggests analytic or global approaches for the student;
- Pinpoints energy highs for each student, facilitating the scheduling of difficult material and some group instruction;
- Offers a basis for designing the classroom to complement each student's style; and
- Indicates the learning methods expected to be most successful for the student (e.g., Contract Activity Packages [CAPs], Programmed Learning Sequences [PLSs], Multisensory Instructional Packages [MIPs], tactile manipulatives, or kinesthetic games, or a combination). For an explanation of these methods, see Chapter 4. For a more complete explanation, refer to Dunn and Dunn 1992, 1993; Dunn, Dunn, and Perrin 1994.

Figure 2.1
Individual Preferences Among Elements and Stimuli Determine Learning Styles

The *LSI* does not measure underlying psychological factors, value systems, or the quality of attitudes. Rather, it yields information about patterns through which learning occurs.

The *Learning Style Inventory: Primary Version (LSI: PV)* (Perrin 1982) is most suitable for students in kindergarten through 2nd grade. The *LSI: PV* is a pictorial assessment of young children's learning styles that should be administered individually. The *LSI: PV* includes a manual that explains how to give the test. Although the questions are posed so that any adult can administer the test and help compile the hand-scorable data, the teacher gains an advantage by administering the *LSI: PV* and gathering information about each child.

The *Learning Style Inventory* for students in grades 3–12 is a result of content and factor analysis (Dunn, Dunn, and Price 1974, 1978, 1984, 1989) and has specific forms for different grade levels that permit analyses of the conditions under which students prefer to learn. The *LSI* is easy to use and interpret, and consists of more than 100 similar items (e.g., "When I really have a lot of studying to do, I like to work alone," and "I enjoy being with friends when I study") that can be completed in 30 to 40 minutes. The *LSI* identifies each student's preferences for 21 elements of style. The items are rated on a five-point Likert scale.

For teachers and other adults, use the *Productivity Environmental Preference Survey (PEPS)* (Dunn, Dunn, and Price 1989; DeBello 1990; and Griggs, Griggs, Dunn, and Ingham 1994). Software is available to help interpret and score this instrument (Dunn and Klavas 1992b; Dunn and Dunn 1992, 1995).

Introduce Learning Styles to Staff and Parents _____

Supervisors are, and should be, the driving force behind educational improvement. Unfortunately, many innovations are paraded before us with far too little time to experiment. So, when the current approach fails to produce across-the-board gains, we discard it and implement the next method—for everyone. Using exactly the same approach to teach everyone is why nothing increases achievement for most students.

In addition, few instructional approaches begin tactilely, kinesthetically, and globally—the primary learning style traits of children who fail reading or math. Few approaches systematically permit global students to learn while sitting informally, in subdued light, with music, while snacking, and as they prefer—alone, in a pair, near their teacher, or in a small group. In short, few approaches differentiate among children's learning styles, and that is why nothing seems to work with failing students.

Consider what happened in the Buffalo City Schools—the second largest urban center in New York:

• In the first year, special education students in the learning style program achieved statistically higher reading and math scores on both the standardized *California Achievement Tests of Basic Skills* and the *Woodcock-Johnson Achievement Tests* than the students in the regular special education program.

• In the second year of the program, the special education students in the learning style program achieved almost as well as the regular education students.

• In the third year, the special education students were placed into inclusion classes and the Buffalo administration challenged visitors to identify which students (K–12) had been in special education. Buffalo uses learning styles throughout the district—not just for youngsters in special education, but also for the gifted, bilingual, and all junior high school students.

With just one hour of extended staff time, I introduced learning styles to my staff. After that, six teachers asked, "Where do we go from here?"

Peter Barrans, Vice Principal, Scarborough, Ontario, Canada

For these reasons, you can introduce learning styles to your faculty and be confident of the results. Teachers have different learning styles, however, so consider each of the following approaches to introduce styles to faculty. Then choose the approach that best fits your style and the styles of your staff.

You don't have to begin in the same way with everyone. Identify the teachers' learning styles with the *Productivity Environmental Preference Survey (PEPS)* (Dunn, Dunn, and Price 1989), then

- Work directly with authority-oriented teachers
- Form a committee of collegial teachers and provide enough leadership for them to begin working together
- Allow teachers who prefer to learn alone to try their own approaches
- Develop a plan for the teachers (and you) to visit classrooms periodically to observe other strategies

Most teachers believe they know what is meant by *learning styles* but they may have different understandings of the construct. Some think the term pertains to modalities, others envision right-brain and left-brain processing, others imagine new classroom environments. If learning styles are to provide a breakthrough toward increased achievement for students, start at the beginning with everyone. Invite teachers, parents, administrators, guidance counselors, attendance officers, psychologists, and student leaders to an initial session to participate in an overview of what teaching-to-styles entails. Require that all instructional administrators and supervisors commit to the practices related to learning styles. Everyone needs to understand and recognize the differences between their own style and those of their colleagues, their spouse, and their children. Once key school personnel realize the many differences among the styles in their own families and among their colleagues, they will recognize the importance of responding to the styles of the children in each class.

Introduce learning style approaches gradually to win supporters and avoid anxiety among overburdened staff and parents. Choose the best alternative for introducing it to your school—given your staff and budget—begin, and consistently move toward specific goals.

Alternative A: Develop Staff Trainers Through Workshops

The best alternative is to train your own staff. Send tenured, mature staff to an in-depth workshop to learn about and experience their own learning styles, observe teachers as they teach the same content using different approaches to respond to diverse styles, and discover how researchers determine the effects of each learning style as they experiment with it and additional styles. The workshop should include information on how to evaluate the effects of learning style practices on individual students and groups of specific students. Minimally, each teacher should leave the workshop knowing how to convert a specific curriculum unit into Contract Activity Packages (CAPs), Programmed Learning Sequences (PLSs), Multisensory Instructional Packages (MIPs), and tactile and kinesthetic instructional resources.

If your school or district invests time, energy, and money in this approach, choose experts with documented success in implementing learning style programs. Consider only fully certified trainers or a university or school center with certified trainers on the faculty. For information, refer to the Resources section under Development Teams.

After the workshop, begin inservice training. Include as many staff, parents, and leadership students in the inservice training as your budget permits—and don't forget yourself. Principals and other supervisors must participate in the training to show commitment and to become learning style educators. Understanding learning styles is the only way to recognize problems and correct misconceptions or inappropriately implemented strategies. Do not hesitate to offer experienced teachers inservice training—especially those who do not generally elect to be innovators. As senior teachers gradually become positive about the practices of learning style, they are likely to convert others. Parents and students can learn to prepare instructional resources, and parents can help prepare students for the assessment and administer the instruments.

Provide in-depth staff development, and your school and district will gain models and nurturers. The on-site trainers will more than reimburse the school system for training costs by providing staff development for everyone else. Trainers act as mentors for new, returning, and substitute teachers, as well as for administrators and parents.

> *In every classroom, the achievement gains of the children using learning styles has convinced teachers to become advocates.*
>
> Duane Alm, Principal, Aberdeen, S.D.

Alternative B: Develop a Self-Teaching Team

Arrange for at least one full day of initial inservice training for the entire staff, but remember that 55 percent of all adults are "morning people," 28 percent are "night owls," and a healthy percentage of your staff will have energy lows in the afternoon. Lead the training yourself, or choose someone else who is liked and supports the program. Develop Team Learning (Dunn and Dunn 1992, 1993; Dunn, Dunn, and Perrin 1994; Dunn and Griggs 1995) by distributing succinct printed material about learning styles for each group of three to five participants. Give each group the opportunity to read the Team Learning material and respond to three different types of related objectives—factual, higher-level cognitive, and creative. The factual objectives ensure that participants understand basic information about style; the higher level cognitive objectives require them to think about the implications of using styles-responsive strategies; and the creative objectives help them apply the information by expressing it in a poem, a crossword puzzle, a game, a tactile manipulative, or any other original instructional resource.

You may choose an experienced trainer to introduce the concept in practical terms and specify strategies for the teachers to implement in stages—during the next week, the next month, and next year. The trainer can help develop an overall implementation time line based on the various stages that need to be incorporated for your staff to follow or alter. See Figure 2.2 for suggestions of the various stages, or Dunn and Dunn 1992 (Chapter 10) and 1993 (Chapter 10) for guidelines.

Encourage participants to identify steps they would take if they agree the concept has potential value. Organize the volunteers into a learning styles implementation committee, and give them all the support you can.

Alternative C: Create a Learning Styles Committee

Establish a committee of teachers, administrators, and parents who are familiar with staff development. Ask each member to experiment with at least two new learning style practices each month, using them several times to increase their own and their students' comfort. This will allow everyone to begin feeling the positive effects of how well students can learn new materials and how enjoyably they respond to the process. As teachers develop expertise with their own or a colleague's class, ask them to share their successes with the entire staff during monthly meetings. As teachers find that a particular practice works for them and certain students, encourage them to help another colleague experiment with that same practice. Suggest that they explain that, although they received basic training, they, too, are just beginning. Advise them to offer collegial assistance rather than authoritative know-how. Little by little, committee members should implement different learning style approaches, discuss and demonstrate them with colleagues, and then explore the next strategy that interests them and is appropriate for their students.

Charge the committee with providing small-group training for other interested teachers, student leaders, administrators, and parents. Easy-to-try practices include a combination of Team Learning to introduce new information and Circle of Knowledge, the small-group strategy for

Figure 2.2
Klavas Implementation Model: A Global Presentation of Implementing Learning Styles

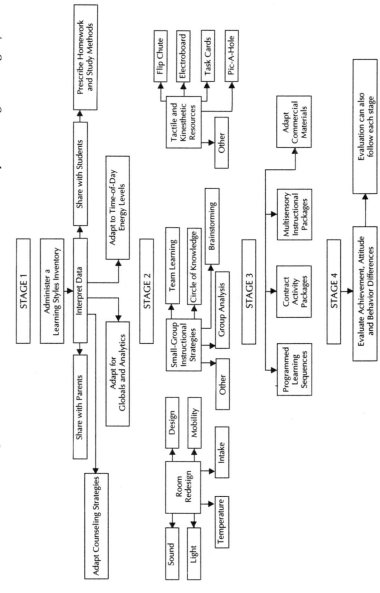

Source: Angela Klavas, St. John's University, Jamaica, New York

peer-oriented students, to reinforce it. Urge committee members to teach learning style approaches to at least eight colleagues each term.

Alternative D: Capitalize on Consultants

If you hire consultants, choose only certified learning style trainers whose implementation efforts show achievement and attitude gains. Certified learning style educators are experienced in all phases of implementation, have successfully used learning style approaches in their classrooms or schools, and have had their resources corrected, revised, and improved. Note that, because of learning style differences, even the best consultant will elicit mixed reactions from your staff—admiration from many, disdain from a few, little response from some, and indifference from others.

Alternative E: Hire a Development Team

Several universities offer teams of professorial and practitioner trainers to help develop group learning styles expertise. These teams are available for one-, two-, three- and five-day workshops at your site. The cost depends on the experience and the number of trainers in the team, the number of staff to be trained, and the number of training days. Teams are available all year (summer included), to help staff and parents develop expertise in all phases of learning style implementation. If you consider this alternative, see Development Teams in the Resources section.

Supplement Learning Style Training

The next steps will help ensure comfort for those involved with the gradual implementation of the learning style approach.

Develop Resources. Guidelines for a perfect set of learning style materials are available in several books (Dunn and Dunn 1992, 1993; Dunn, Dunn, and Perrin 1994). Develop these resources on computers for easy duplication, distribution, and adaptation. Appoint good grammarians and hire expert trainers to correct original instructional resources, and then offer teachers easy access to the materials.

Obtain Resources. Collect a few how-to books, videotapes, audiotapes, computer programs, and tactile and kinesthetic resources for the people involved in learning style training. Circulate the resources and solicit frequent individual feedback. See Resources for a variety of media.

Gather Feedback. Within two days of any introductory workshop, send a survey to participants.

Ask Teachers

• To what extent are you interested in trying a few learning style strategies? Scale: 1 = barely interested; 5 = very interested.
• Would you participate in a meeting on learning style training, if we assure you that you can stop the process if your first steps are ineffective?
• Would you like to have your learning style identified?
• Would you like to have your spouse's learning style identified?
• Would you like to have your child's learning style identified?
• Would you like to have the learning styles of students in one of your classes identified? If so, how many students are in that class?
• If you would like your students' styles identified, would you prepare them to take a learning style assessment by reading a short story with them and discussing the construct? Or, would you prefer a parent to prepare your students for the assessment?

Ask Parents

• To what extent are you interested in having your child exposed to learning style strategies? Scale: 1 = barely interested; 5 = very interested.

- Would you like to have your learning style identified? Your spouse's?
- Would you be willing to pay $1.25 for each (adult) assessment?
- Would you like to have your child's learning style identified?
- Would you be willing to assist a teacher in preparing a class for taking a learning style inventory? (It requires reading a short story with the students and discussing the concept with them.)
- Would you be willing to prepare a class for taking a learning style inventory without the assistance of a teacher? (If so, we will discuss what needs to be done.)

The survey responses will help you determine how many teachers and parents are willing to begin working with learning styles. Schedule a meeting and lead it yourself, or select a capable and interested staff member as chair. Help the group develop skills for preparing students for a learning styles assessment by discussing learning style and taking their own inventories. Charge the chair to

1. Administer the instruments.
2. Process the tests.
3. Identify each person's learning style.
4. a. Schedule a meeting for the participants to receive and discuss their results.
   b. Schedule interested teachers' classes for learning style assessment.
   c. Secure the copies of the stories and assessments appropriate for those students. (See Connecting Learning Styles and Students in Chapter 3.)

Do not distribute the stories to uninterested staff.

3
Stepping into the Classroom

BECAUSE INSTRUCTION THAT RECOGNIZES CHILDREN'S LEARNING
styles helps them to be the very best they can be,
supervisors should encourage teachers to experiment with
learning style instruction. A supervisor educated in learning
styles is a valuable mentor and can help teachers choose
the steps and sequences for their classes. But the success
of the program ultimately rests with the teachers and their
students. Just as teachers need to respect students'
learning styles, supervisors need to respect teachers'
teaching styles. Teachers are the impetus for learning styles
from this step on.

Connecting Learning Styles and Students

Introduce learning styles to students by explaining the
different styles that exist among all classrooms of students,
families, and cultures. Tell students that their mother's style
is likely to be different from their father's style, and that
their style is probably different from friends' and
classmates' styles.

Students need to understand that everyone has
strengths, but that each person's strengths are different.
Explain to them that learning styles are based on complex
reactions to many different things in their lives, including
feelings, routines, and events. As a result, patterns often
develop and repeat whenever anyone concentrates on new
and difficult material. Introduce the idea of learning about
their strengths by honestly answering a series of questions
that will be assessed, not graded. Explain that only honest

> *Our summer learning style program offered only 18 days of instruction, but many students accomplished goals that they hadn't mastered through years of traditional education.*
>
> Sherrye Dotson, Director of Secondary Instruction,
> Jacksonville, Texas

answers will result in information that will make it easier for them to learn.

Discuss different learning styles thoroughly with the class, regardless of grade level. Then choose an age-appropriate book about learning styles to share with the class. The following stories legitimatize different styles and explain that there is no such thing as a good or a bad style.

• *Elephant Style* (Perrin and Santora 1982) for kindergarten through 2nd grade. Two friendly elephants, Ellie and Fonty, love to play together, but are not able to learn in the same way in school. (This book accompanies the *Learning Style Inventory: Primary Version.*)

• *Kids in Style* (Lenehan 1991) for kindergarten through grades 4. This book explains the concept of global and analytic processing.

• *Mission from No-Style* (Braio 1988) for grades 3–6. Space children and earthlings join in a search for information on how to learn new and difficult information. Together they unravel the mystery of how to achieve well in school.

• *Return to No-Style* (Braio 1990) for special education students in grades 3–6. Imaginary characters, designed to intrigue slowly achieving youngsters, are used to describe the concept of learning style.

• *Two-of-a-Kind Learning Styles* (Pena 1989) for grades 5–8. Two middle school students, Global Myrna and Analytic Victor, enjoy their leisure activities together, but must study separately because of the differences between their learning styles.

- *A Guide to Explaining Learning Styles to High School Students* (Bouwman 1991) for grades 9–12. This guide helps older students develop an understanding of learning styles, and helps them interpret their own styles.

If it's necessary to read the story to young students, tape record it and indicate when a listener should turn the page. (This strategy can help primary students learn to read by matching the sounds with the words in the book.) Break the tab on the tape to prevent accidental erasure and glue the cassette's box to the back of the book. Allow students access to the book, tape, and tape player during free time and after finishing assignments.

Assessing Your Students

Assess each student's learning style, either by experimenting with tactile and kinesthetic resources and various environments, or by administering an inventory. Each inventory includes instructions for administering, scoring, and interpreting the data.

If you choose the *LSI,* the *Homework Disc Software Package* can help you interpret the assessments. It provides ideas on how students can use learning styles to understand and remember information that is new and difficult. This software supplies individual study and homework prescriptions, and gives tips on the best environment and resources for each student (Dunn and Klavas 1992a).

Strengthening Students' Understanding of Learning Styles

After assessing and prescribing practices for each student, identify which elements of style affect large clusters of students in the class and select learning style approaches that match their needs. Develop one wall chart that indicates each student's strong preferences (scores of between 20–30 or 70–80 on the *LSI,* or scores of 5 on the *LSI: PV*), and a second chart that shows how to best use their preferences when working on assignments either at home or in the classroom.

Encourage students to predict the styles of their family members by describing behaviors that suggest characteristics of learning styles. Direct the students to survey their relatives to see how accurately they guessed, and then compare their family's styles with the styles of their classmates' families. They can illustrate their guesses about learning styles, and write poems or stories about how they feel about their *LSI* results.

After testing students, we schedule a general meeting with the parents and explain how to interpret the LSI. The results help students, teachers, and families understand each other.

Sister Natalie Lafser, Director, St. Louis, Mo.

Students will have difficulty using their styles for completing assignments and homework until they learn how to teach themselves tactilely and kinesthetically. So, it may be practical to begin by teaching the students to develop their own Electroboards, Flip Chutes, Pic-A-Holes, Multipart Task Cards, and kinesthetic floor games (Dunn and Dunn 1992, 1993; Dunn, Dunn, and Perrin 1994; Dunn and Griggs 1995). See Chapter 4 for descriptions of these instructional strategies that effectively teach tactile learners to absorb difficult information through their perceptual strength— their tactile modality.

Meanwhile, teachers should share the learning styles results with students' parents. Discuss their child's learning style, and the learning style shared by the majority of that child's classmates. Explain to parents and to students what the learning style guidelines mean, and how to use them. Ask parents to encourage their children to use their learning styles.

Personalize Learning Styles

Use students' learning styles in conjunction with the *Klavas Implementation Model* (Figure 2.2) to help choose your first approach to using learning styles. The model illustrates stages used in successful learning style programs. Adjust the model to suit your teachers' teaching styles and risk-taking tolerance, recognizing that they do not need to implement every stage. Proceed slowly so that both your teachers and their students are comfortable and successful in each stage. The model is a result of research on factors that helped or hindered learning style programs in several regions of the United States (Klavas, Dunn, Griggs, Gemake, Geisert, and Zenhausern 1994).

The model is a flow chart of choices designed to incrementally contribute to increased student achievement, improved attitudes toward school, and better behavior. Examine it and the ideas listed below, and then help your teachers implement the best ones for their classrooms:

- Enlist guidance counselors, school psychologists, and parents to encourage students to follow their learning style prescriptions.
- Influence class scheduling, if you can, by assigning difficult subjects and formidable tests during energy highs. For example, experiment with scheduling students to take the SATs during their energy highs. If SAT schedules must be altered, send a request to Educational Testing Services on school stationery.
- Urge teachers to encourage students to study at their best time of day by explaining their chronobiological highs. Allow for some leisure activities during their lows.
- Suggest that teachers experiment with introducing topics globally followed by analytic reinforcement; reverse the sequence the next day. Remind them to explain the difference between the two processing styles to help students become more aware of their own style, and understand why they react in a certain way to each lesson. Ask teachers to note which students perform best and seem most interested during the global versus the analytic introductions. (Most teachers and textbooks present

> *Twenty-two junior high school teenagers signed a scrawled note asking whom to thank for teaching their teachers about learning styles.*
>
> Dorothy Logan-Alexander, Assistant Superintendent,
> Brookhaven, Miss.

materials analytically, so be certain that they know how to teach globally.) Teaching both analytically and globally is one of the most important elements of style.

When teachers feel comfortable responding to at least some of the elements of learning styles that are important to their students (Figure 2.2, Stage 2), they should share their experiences with the students' parents and encourage the parents to use learning styles with their younger children (Dunn, Dunn, and Treffinger 1992).

4
Personalizing Learning

SUGGEST THAT TEACHERS EXPERIMENT WITH REDESIGNING THEIR classroom, from the physical environment to the learning methods, in Stage 2 of the *Klavas Implementation Model* (Figure 2.2 on page 21). Encourage them to choose the ideas to implement, and to begin in any order practical for them and their students. In deciding where to start, teachers should factor in their students' assessments, and their own comfort with each idea.

Redesigning Conventional Classrooms

With a basic understanding of styles and needs, students can redesign the classroom. Teachers should help them compile a list of adjustments that respond to their own and their classmates' learning style differences. One way to begin classroom redesign is to have the students measure the available furniture and then create paper representations to cut out and move around on a scaled floor plan of the classroom. They can use cardboard boxes, plants, bricks, yarn, and other readily available materials to make dens, offices, and nooks. Teachers should guide students by showing them illustrations of other learning style classrooms.

Students enjoy rearranging furniture, whether they focus on one area or the whole classroom (Figures 4.1 and 4.2).When at least one space appeals to each learner, encourage teachers and students to test that floor plan for a week. New designs can be considered after testing the first ideas. Together with your teachers, compare behavior problems and incomplete assignments with previous

Figure 4.1
Begin Classroom Redesign With Dividers
Between Quiet and Active Areas

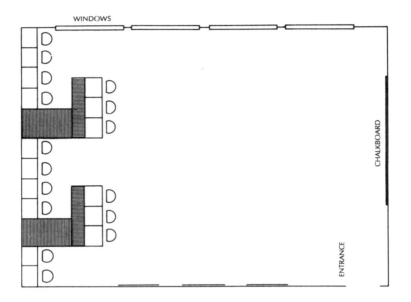

Reprinted with permission (Dunn and Dunn 1992)

occurrences, and ask the students about their new environment, and their grades before and after the change. Students usually love the new environment and rarely permit teachers to return to a conventional environment without challenge.

When your teachers decide to experiment with the physical classroom, remind them to consider several physiological and sociological aspects of learning. Factors include seating, lighting, sound, temperature, attention spans, and particular group or individual learning arrangements. If teachers have several students who require informal seating, suggest that they begin the transition into style with seating arrangements; if they have

Figure 4.2
Continue Classroom Redesign Using Dividers to Separate Independent Workers from Students Needing Supervision

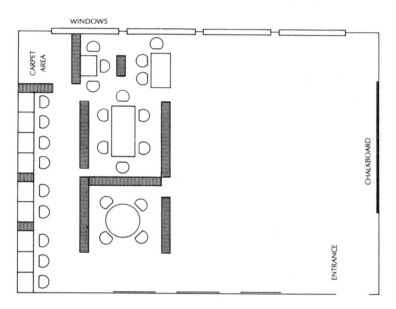

Reprinted with permission (Dunn and Dunn 1992)

a cluster of students who need soft illumination, suggest changes in lighting.

Seating. Most schools provide a combination of chairs, desks, and tables made of wood, steel, and plastic for each student. Resting on that inflexible surface is about four square inches of bone that supports 75 percent of a student's total body weight (Shea 1983). The result? Physical discomfort that becomes a distraction—squirming, fidgeting, rocking—and, eventually, a need to get out of the chair.

Many students achieve better when they are allowed to use cushions on either their chairs or the floor, sit on beanbags or other casual furniture, or relax in a carpeted,

> *Students achieved higher scores on the* Iowa Basic Skills Tests *in both reading and math when we tested them at their best time of day and in a relaxed environment. Students remembered facts more easily and more confidently when taught in their style.*
>
> Patricia Lemmon, Retired Principal, Hutchinson, Kan.

informal section of the room (Hodges 1985, Shea 1983, Nganwa-Bagumah 1986, and Nganwa-Bagumah and Mwamwenda 1991). Relaxing while concentrating is more crucial for global students and adolescents than for either analytic primary or elementary students for whom it also may be important (Dunn 1987, Dunn and Griggs 1988). To acquire more comfortable and suitable seating arrangements, ask parents to donate cushions, beanbag chairs, carpet squares, rugs, outdoor furniture, couches, rocking chairs, or easy chairs.

Lighting. Although fluorescent lights are used in most classrooms, they have negative effects on some students. The fade time of florescent lighting is longer than 50 percent of the cycle time, is worse with old bulbs than with new bulbs, and cycles 60 times a second. That reverse phasing stimulates analytics who find it difficult to concentrate on demanding academics in low light, and overstimulates global processors who tend to react with restlessness and

> *Our decor is early Salvation Army, but no one seems to mind. Students make their own decisions about where in the classroom and with whom to work.*
>
> Mary Laffey, Principal, Columbia, Mo.

hyperactivity. Reducing illumination results in higher test scores for children who prefer soft illumination (Dunn, Krimsky, Murray, and Quinn 1985).

Ott (1973) reported the positive and negative effects of natural versus artificial light on plants. The identical exposure was beneficial for some and detrimental to others. People also respond differently to lighting. To find the optimum lighting for students, teachers may try one or more of the following experiments for six weeks:

- Use only half of the lights in the classroom. Permit students to sit wherever they feel most comfortable. Or turn the lights off in one corner, and encourage poor readers to sit there. Ask teachers to note differences in behavior and attention spans, and watch for changes in achievement.
- Encourage poor readers to choose a piece of colored acetate (often used on overhead projectors), and to place it on each page of their book, moving it from page to page. Look for changes in attention span, focussing, and behavior. Expect improvement in 5 to 10 percent of poor readers.
- Insert colored, fireproof paper between light bulbs and covers in one or more areas of the classroom. (Find fireproof paper in greeting card stores.)
- Teach in natural light. Teachers may not appreciate the atmosphere, but many students will!
- Permit students to wear sun visors, sunglasses, or caps with visors if they ask or their *LSI* shows a score of 40 or below on light. Adults require more light than children, and bright lights cause tension in some students (Studd 1995).
- Cover large, bright white surfaces whenever possible.
- Use dark curtains to shade areas for students who need soft illumination, or allow students to partly shade their working areas with transparent, dark-toned fabrics.

Sound. The ability to concentrate on difficult cognitive tasks in either quiet or noise varies among individuals (Pizzo, Dunn, and Dunn 1990). Strongly analytic processors require quiet, whereas strongly global processors often think better with sound, including music, modified background conversations, ocean waves crashing, or birds singing. For students who strongly prefer background noise (*LSI* scores of 60 or higher on noise), use only music without lyrics because the mind automatically repeats lyrics instead of concentrating on tasks.

Encourage teachers and students to experiment with sound:

- Encourage students who need quiet to sit away from traffic and activity patterns.
- Allow soft cotton or rubber ear plugs, joggers' earmuffs, or nonfunctioning headphones during tests or in study environments.
- Carpet the traffic areas for the 10 to 12 percent of students distracted by sound.
- Provide private classroom spaces for students distracted by noise.
- Offer seats near the hub of activities or the door for students who require noise.
- Permit music on headphones for students who prefer background noise.

Temperature. In every group of people, some members feel warm and others feel cool—and everyone else is comfortable. Temperature preferences are unrelated to either global or analytic processing, but need to be accommodated for learning efficiency. Responding to strong temperature preferences improves achievement (Dunn and Dunn 1992, 1993; Dunn, Dunn, and Perrin 1994). Students who seem devoid of energy or consistently withdrawn may be experiencing environmental discomfort. The following measures may help some students:

- Use curtains to block out the sun and drafts.
- Turn on a fan, and let students choose their seats.
- Supply paper cups and water for drinking, and dabbing on faces and wrists.
- Allow students to keep a sweater in their desks or in a closet.
- Encourage students to layer their clothing so they can put on or take off items.

- Remember that the warmest part of a room is in the middle—with weather-dependent exceptions near windows and heat sources.

Attention Spans. Some students have a strong emotional need to work on a task until it is done. These youngsters often concentrate in uninterrupted periods and are most often analytic processors. In contrast, global processors tend to begin a task with a burst of energy, work for a short period of time, and then take a break. And, they dislike to work on one thing at a time, preferring to engage in multiple tasks.

Classrooms need to accommodate both global and analytic processors. Help arrange classrooms to permit analytics a section without noise, people, or other distractions and offer global processors diversified activities, projects, and interactions. Instructional environments need to include both settings to help all students succeed academically.

- Arrange desks and chairs in dens, alcoves, and private spaces so other students do not disturb analytic processors.
- Find seating that accommodates the differences among students' height, weight, and girth to alleviate distractions caused by discomfort.
- Allow students to stand or sit casually while concentrating and completing assignments.
- Designate an aisle or section of the room for kinesthetic students to walk quietly while they read, complete tasks, and think.
- Structure assignments to permit variety, mobility, breaks, and peer interaction for students who need breaks. Allow these students to move around the room as they study, switch activities, and migrate purposefully from one area to another.
- Designate small-group work areas.
- Allot areas for global students to engage in a variety of short, instructional activities and for analytics to work without interruption. Adjust lights, seats, and acoustics in these areas to allow for mobility and social interactions. It is

possible to develop these nontraditional spaces without much effort, time, or money (Dunn and Dunn 1992, 1993).

Sociological Preferences. The social setting in which children learn best is incidental to their global or analytic tendencies. Many children learn best in a mixture of patterns—sometimes alone, in a pair, in a small group of peers, in a team, with an authoritative or collegial teacher. An individual's sociological patterns may vary with age and achievement. Some people learn consistently in one way, others in varied patterns, and still others have no preference. However, more global students than analytic students are peer-oriented (Dunn, Cavanaugh, Eberle, and Zenhausern 1982). Peer-oriented children often learn best with either a single friend or in a small group, in contrast to 13 percent of all students who learn best alone, and the 28 percent who need a teacher. Let students choose the social setting to complete all or most assignments, with the exception of tests, until they or their teachers determine that the setting is inappropriate.

Rules for Learning Styles Privileges

The benefits of experimenting with the physical classroom far outweigh any imagined risks, but teachers must establish firm ground rules that even the youngest students can understand. List ground rules on a wall chart and illustrate them for global students, see Figure 4.3 on page 39. Start with basic rules, and add others as they become important. Teachers should emphasize that practicing their learning styles includes the use of certain privileges, but that disregarding rules will result in losing privileges.

The ground rules change with the privileges being introduced. For example, introducing intake (water and raw vegetables) may require a rule that intake is allowed in your classroom but not necessarily in other teachers' classrooms.

Redesigning Teaching Strategies

Match teaching strategies with the learning style profile of each student. No single approach will be effective with all

Figure 4.3

Rules for Using Learning Styles Privileges

(1) Your learning style must not distract anyone else. **SHHHHHHHHHH**

(2) Your grades must improve. B → **B+**

(3) Your assignments must be completed on time.

December 1995						
Sunday	Monday	Tuesday	Wednesday	Thursday	Friday	Saturday
					1	2
3	4	5	6	7	8	9
10	11	12	13	14	15	16
17	18	19	20	21	22	23
24	25	26	27	28	29	30
31						

(4) Whenever I need your attention, you must give it to me immediately.

(5) The way you work in class is based on your learning style assessment and subsequent evaluations.

*Your
Learning
Style*

A. Student
March 1998

students, but allow students to experiment with several methods to identify which are interesting and help them understand difficult material most easily. After a few experiences with each method, students should choose the method that most benefits them.

Tactile and Kinesthetic Resources

Students who perform poorly in a conventional school often have tactile or kinesthetic strengths, but are required to learn by listening (auditorially) or by reading (visually). These and other students need to learn how to teach themselves by using Multipart Task Cards, Flip Chutes, Pic-A-Holes, Electroboards, and floor games (Dunn and Dunn 1992, 1993; Dunn, Dunn, and Perrin 1994; Dunn and Griggs 1995). Every time new and difficult material is introduced, students should create and use these manipulatives so that they value the resources, learn at least one method for teaching themselves, and have at least one strategy for becoming successful academically.

Task Cards

Multipart Task Cards are easy-to-make, self-corrective, tactile and visual resources that help many students who do remember easily by listening or by reading. Task Cards are effective in introducing new material and in reinforcing material.

Students who use Task Cards may work at their desk, or anywhere in the school or home. Task Cards may be used by individuals, or in a pair, or in a small group—provided that everyone follows the rules.

Task Cards present information about a specific topic, concept, or skill that has been translated into either questions and answers or sample answers (some true, some false). A student can make Task Cards by (1) printing the name of each state in the United States on the left side of an index card, (2) printing the name of the state's capitol in the middle, and (3) gluing a picture of the state's outline (or famous product) on the right side of the card. Then, they cut the card into irregularly shaped thirds so that only the correct answers fit together.

Flip Chutes

Make Flip Chutes from half-gallon orange juice or milk containers. Design small question-and-answer cards to insert into the upper face of the container. As each question card descends on an inner slide, it flips over and emerges from a lower opening, displaying the answer. Decorate the container with a paint, contact paper, and lettering that relate to the topic.

Pic-A-Holes

Use this method to introduce or reinforce information for tactile students. A Pic-A-Hole includes a series of cards, each with one question and three possible answers printed near the bottom. The student inserts a golf tee into the hole directly below the answer chosen. If the question card lifts from the holder with the tee in place, the answer is correct.

Electroboards

Electroboards consistently hold the attention of most students. Immediate visual feedback is provided by a bulb that lights up when an answer is correct. Questions are on one side of the Electroboard, and the answers are out of sequence on the other. Students use a two-prong continuity tester to choose a question on one side and the answer on the other. The right answer illuminates the bulb.

Electroboards and all other tactile resources are particularly inviting if the outer shapes reflect the subject. For example, make an Electroboard in the shape of a whale.

Floor Games

Buy a large sheet of plastic or use old tablecloths, shower curtains, carpet remnants, or sails on which to glue, draw, or decorate with a game designed to let students hop, jump, or move around as they are exposed to the major or finer points of the topic through questions or tasks. A popular commercial floor game, although rudimentary in this context, causes players to stretch across a floor mat (and each other) to reach spots of colors as dictated by the spins of a color wheel.

> *In one year of using learning styles, teachers noted major gains in student performance and attitude. In just a few weeks, I noticed that teachers using learning styles had fewer discipline problems than teachers using traditional methods.*
>
> Mary Fisher, Principal, Winner, S.D.

Small-Group Instruction

Another strategy teachers can implement is small-group instruction. About 28 percent of students are peer-oriented, although many can learn with one or more classmates at least some of the time. Thus, as a transition from teacher-directed instruction, experiment with Team Learning to introduce difficult new information, Circle of Knowledge to reinforce it, and brainstorming to develop problem-solving skills. Unlike cooperative learning, which requires teacher-directed learning followed by students learning together, these approaches allow peer-oriented students to teach themselves or each other without direct teacher involvement.

Team Learning. Use the Team Learning approach to permit students to learn the most difficult information in any unit or topic independently, in a pair, or in a small group. Give each topic a name that describes the subject, for example. "Team Learning: Who Do You Think You Are? Digging for Family Roots." Then, list the names of each student, if they work in a group, and identify the recorder. Teach the students what they need to know to master the objective of the lesson, and then follow with the three types of questions: factual, higher-level cognitive, and creative.

A factual question might be to explain the meaning of genealogy and use and spell the word correctly in a sentence. A higher-level cognitive question doesn't have a right or wrong answer, but it requires students to hypothesize and analyze. A teacher may ask students to list five advantages and disadvantages of tracing a family's genealogy. Follow those questions with one that requires the creative application of the information that is being learned. For example, ask students to write a humorous poem that describes what might happen when people trace their family trees.

After answering these questions, the teacher should have the students share their answers with the rest of the class.

Circle of Knowledge. Teachers use Circle of Knowledge to reinforce new and difficult material directly related to the objectives in the Team Learning, introduced a day or two before. As in Team Learning, name the topic and the students participating, and identify the recorder. Students may choose to work alone, in a pair, or in groups of three of four. Students who work together should work in a small circle. The teacher poses a single question or objective, and the members of each group work together, developing possible answers. The method for answering is a clockwise rotation of answers, until time is called or the members have exhausted their ideas. When time is up, the groups share their answers with the teacher who writes them on the chalkboard. The class analyzes the answers; scores result from a mixture of unique and correct answers, and challenges of incorrect answers.

Contract Activity Packages (CAPs)

Use this strategy to let motivated students progress at their own speed and avoid the repetition and interruptions inherent in large-group instruction. CAPs are also effective with nonconforming students who often fail to do what their teachers require in class. Introduce one or two CAPs to the whole class to help students who are motivated, have auditory or visual preferences, or who are nonconforming (Dunn and Dunn, 1992, 1993; Dunn, Dunn, and Perrin 1994).

Contract Activity Packages include
• A simply stated objective.
• Multisensory Resource Alternatives that teach the required information through perceptual preferences.

- Activity Alternatives in which students use the new information to create a Programmed Learning Sequence; a Flip Chute, Multipart Task Cards, Electroboards, Pic-A-Holes, or other tactile resources; floor games or other kinesthetic resources; compositions, poems, plays, scripts, songs, drawings, dances, or pantomimes.
- Reporting alternatives in which students share their creative Activity Alternative.
- Opportunity to work in a social group, usually with more than one peer. CAPs may be used independently.
- Test to assess the student's knowledge of the objective before, during, or after the activity.

Programmed Learning Sequences (PLSs)

Use a PLS for students who prefer learning (a) with structure (b) alone or in a pair, (c) auditorially (d) visually (print or illustrations) (e) tactilely, and (f) in small steps with immediate reinforcement.

A typical Programmed Learning Sequence presents only one idea or fact at a time, requires students to be active learners, and provides immediate feedback. Students may not continue to the next frame until mastering each phase (each phase is sequentially more difficult). After six or seven frames, material is reinforced through tactile resources, and each PLS also has a tape for auditory learners.

Each PLS covers a topic, concept, or skill, and is named appropriately with a humorous subtitle (Math: Divide and Conquer!). Important components include specific directions, a global beginning, and a story woven through the PLS, step-by-step sequencing, and answers.

Multisensory Instructional Packages (MIPs)

Students who do not enjoy school and who resist learning invariably achieve better than before when using MIPs. Although MIPs include a variety of multisensory resources, taped directions sequence the learning according to the user's learning style. Thus, based on each individual's learning style strengths, directions will indicate which resources should be used to begin, reinforce, and review the curriculum. Slow learners find this approach easy to use independently. The directions are personalized and every resource is self-corrective. A tape guides the student through each MIP, and the package includes an Electroboard, Flip Chute, Pic-A-Hole, Task Cards, floor game, and a PLS (Dunn and Dunn 1992, 1993; Dunn, Dunn, and Perrin 1994; Dunn and Griggs 1995).

Realistic Goals and Evaluations

It may take three years to fully implement learning style instruction within a school. Concentrate only on learning styles during that entire period. Provide support and encouragement to those who experiment. Introduce and continue at least one new learning styles approach each week or two, until it is comfortable for both teachers and students.

Use the *Klavas Implementation Model* (Figure 2.2 on page 21) as a guide. Stage 1 should be completed within four months; Stage 2 will take another six months. Within the first year, identify students' styles, share them with children and parents, provide homework prescriptions, teach lessons globally, introduce tactile and kinesthetic resources, use three small-group strategies, and redesign the classroom. The second year, add CAPs and PLSs. The third year, continue experimenting with these approaches and gradually add MIPs and other strategies that have not yet been introduced.

How to Track Learning Styles

Tracking available materials and learning styles is easy if you develop a code for each instructional resource, and insert that code into your lesson plan. For example, insert a *C* to indicate that a Contract Activity Package may be used to teach the lesson's objective. Remember that it isn't necessary to respond to every student's style in every lesson, but that it is helpful to compare achievement when they use their styles and when they don't. Comparing helps verify each student's assessment and best learning style.

Here's a sample of codes, along with the students who most benefit from using each material:

C = CAP for independent, nonconforming, yet motivated students who are either auditory or visual learners.

P = PLS for students who need structure and are either visual or tactile and motivated.

T = Tactile resources for tactile students.

K = Kinesthetic resources for kinesthetic resources.

M = Multisensory Instructional Packages for students with low perceptual preferences in all modalities and short attention spans.

S = Small-group techniques for peer-oriented students.

A = Assignments, with subcategories for students with different intelligences, including *Ap* for poetry, *Acwp* for a crossword puzzle, *Ac* for a composition, and *Apd* for a panel discussion.

Win Your Community

Studies by independent researchers and faculty at more than 100 colleges and universities corroborate learning style differences and the positive effects of providing matched resources, methods, and teaching styles (St. John's University's Center for the Study of Learning and Teaching Styles 1996).You know that, but how do you win support from the community and keep the positive momentum going in your school?

• Share your research with the community. Explain learning styles and how they vary within families.

• Emphasize that all students in the same class are learning the same curriculum—and the same amount of curriculum. The only difference is that they are learning through different instructional resources.

• Test families and everyone who wants to be tested—custodians, secretaries, parents, grandparents— and explain their results.

• Entice the community—involve parents, grandparents, and senior citizens into making CAPs, PLSs, MIPs, and tactile and kinesthetic resources. Ask them to help children create their own resources. Hold workshops on how to develop preschoolers' ability to read by capitalizing on their learning styles (see Dunn, Dunn, and Perrin 1994, Chapter 4).

- Encourage more teachers to experiment with learning styles.
- Form a committee of volunteer teachers and parents to serve as models and educate others.
- Enlist students to train other students.
- Publish the results of the program, don't just brag. Give visitors—and provide reporters—a one- to two-page newsworthy description of the program with testimonials from students, parents, and teachers. Offer clear, black-and-white photographs of students using tactile and kinesthetic resources, engaging in small-group strategies, and learning identical information from very different resources. Identify each student and explain the action in the photo. Do not allow visitors to take photos. (Obtain written permission from adults and parents or guardians for the use of photos and testimonials.)
- Display wall charts with rules for using learning styles strengths. This reminds and guides your students, and reinforces information with visitors.
- Track the progress of learning styles implementation. Focus on learning styles for three years to avoid stressing analytic teachers and to allow the nurturing of global students. Recognize everyone's efforts, reinforce strategies, and observe progress.
- Cite the research. See References and Resources sections for information that interests you.

How to Ensure Success

Encourage the use of learning styles and provide support whenever you can. Generate support from

- Observing, assisting, and praising teachers involved in learning styles
- Sharing successes and ideas
- Recognizing volunteers and the staff at large in implementing strategies
- Comparing the achievement of students (a) whose styles are used in a lesson with the achievement of students whose styles are not used in that lesson; (b) when their

> *In the beginning, parents express concern about kids learning on the floor and snacking while studying. Once they understand the program, they help redesign the room, make tactile materials, and ask to have their other children tested for learning styles.*
>
> Penny Todd Claudis, Curriculum Supervisor and Learning Styles Coordinator, Shreveport, La.

styles are responded to and not; and (c) whose teachers are using learning styles strategies versus the achievement of students in other classes

Bottom-Line Expectations

Teach your students to develop and use tactile and kinesthetic resources. Allow global students to learn informally and in soft lighting. Adjust for sociological preferences. Consistently introduce new and difficult information using tactile or kinesthetic instructional resources, Team Learning, Circle of Knowledge, CAPs, PLSs or MIPs, and underachievers will perform significantly better. Based on a quarter of a century of learning styles experience, I promise that your gifted students will enjoy school more and become increasingly independent learners as they learn how to use CAPs and PLSs, redesign the classroom, and learn as they prefer socially. As these students' attitudes and behaviors improve, their parents will laud your efforts and more people will embrace learning styles.

Read as much as you can, attend workshops, participate in learning styles meetings, encourage experimentation, and exercise flexibility. You and the school must commit to learning styles because introductory workshops with little reinforcement and no long-term commitment discourage everyone. You will never regret implementing learning styles. Perhaps for the first time, you will fully understand what supervisors, administrators, and teachers must do to provide an excellent education for learners with widely diverse styles, interests, talents, temperaments, and personalities. I hope we meet one day so that you can share with me how learning styles gradually changed your concept of a good education.

Resources

Learning Style Schools Open to Visitors

Many schools around the world have reversed poor student achievement by responding to students' learning styles. The educators below are successful implementors who graciously invite readers to visit their schools and observe learning style programs firsthand. I strongly recommend visiting one of these schools.

Michael Adams, Director, The American School of Mozambique, Mozambique, Africa

Duane Alm, Principal, C.C. Lee Elementary School, Aberdeen School District 6-1, Aberdeen, SD 57402-4203. Phone: (605) 622-7157

Jeanette Bowen, Special Education Coordinator, District #24, P.S. 199 Queens, 39-20 48th Avenue, Long Island City, NY 11104. Phone: (718) 784-3431

Carolyn Brunner, Coordinator, Erie 1 BOCES International Learning Styles Center, Maryvale 9/10 Building, 1050 Maryvale Drive, Cheektowaga, NY 14225. Phone: (716) 631-2893

Penny Claudis, Learning Styles Coordinator, Caddo Schools, 1961 Midway Street, P.O. Box 32000, Shreveport, LA 71130-2000. Phone: (318) 636-0210

Ray Cooley, Principal, Junior High School #93, 430 Southside Parkway, Buffalo, NY 14210. Phone: (716) 828-4818

Wanda Dean, Principal, Oxford Elementary School, 1637 Highway 30 E, Oxford, MS 38655. Phone: (601) 234-3497

Joan DellaValle, Principal, Otsego Elementary School, 55 Otsego Street, Dix Hills, NY 11746. Phone: (516) 595-2760

Jim DiSebastian, High School Principal, The American School of Tegucigalpa, Tegucigalpa, Honduras

Sherrye Dotson, District Curriculum Coordinator, Administration Building, Jacksonville Public Schools, Jacksonville, TX 75766. Phone: (903) 586-7208

Larry Howie, Teacher, John A. McManus Elementary School, Chico Unified School District, 988 East Avenue, Chico, CA 95928-5999. Phone: (916) 891-3128

Penjiran Hajah Rahmah Pengiran Haji Jadid, Professor, 11, Villa Sejahtera, Simpang 528, Sungai Hanching, Julan Muara, Brunei Darussalam 3890

Bart Kelliher, Director of Special Education and Special Services, The Buffalo City Schools, 816 City Hall, Buffalo, NY 14202. Phone: (716) 851-3746

Paula and Vic Koshuta, HC 77 #3003, Lowman, ID 83637

Mary Laffey, Principal, Oakland Junior High School, Columbia Public Schools, 3405 Oakland Place, Columbia, MS 65202. Phone: (314) 886-2710

Sister Natalie Lafser, Director, Office of Learning Styles, Saint Louis Archdiocese, 449 South Spring Avenue, St. Louis, MO 63116-4322. Phone: (314) 351-9097

Raja and·Auvo Marckwort, MARCKWORT Training for Corporate Adults, Koulutusyhtiot, Korkeavuorenkatu 41 A 12, 00130 Helsinki, Finland. Phone: 607166. Fax: 358-0-611531

Jan Meritt, Science Teacher, Klammath Union High School, 1300 Montclaire Street, Klammath Falls, OR 97601. Phone: (503) 883-4714

Nancy Murphree, Mathematics Department Chair, Jacksonville Middle School, Jacksonville, TX 75766. Phone: (903) 586-7208

Denise Parker, Developmental Reading Teacher, Oakland Junior High School, Columbia Public Schools, 3405 Oakland Place, Columbia, MO 65202. Phone: (314) 886-2710

Richard Quinn, Associate Superintendent, The Buffalo City Schools, 816 City Hall, Buffalo, NY 14202. Phone: (716) 831-3588

Jody Sands Taylor, Adjunct Professor, University of Virginia, 1008 West Franklin Street, Richmond, VA 23220. Phone: (804) 355-2033 or (804) 872-5411

Fred Thompson, Director, Mazapan School, Le Ceiba, Honduras

Sue Wellman, Science Teacher, Elm Lawn Elementary School, Middleton-Cross Plains Area Schools, 6701 Woodgate Road, Middleton, WI 53562. Phone: (608) 828-1660

Mary E. White, Mathematics Teacher, Oak Martin Middle School, 5650 Cahaba Valley Road Birmingham, AL 35242. Phone: (205) 980-3660

Development Teams

If you decide to employ a consultant or development team, contact the following people for more information:

Carolyn Brunner, Coordinator, Erie 1 BOCES International Learning Styles Center, Maryvale 9/10 Building, 1050 Maryvale Drive, Cheektowaga, NY 14225. Phone: (716) 631-2893

Penny Claudis, Learning Styles Coordinator, Caddo Schools, 1961 Midway Street, P.O. Box 32000, Shreveport, LA 71130-2000. Phone: (318) 636-0210

Wanda Dean, Principal, Oxford Elementary School, 1637 Highway 30 E, Oxford, MS 38655. Phone: (601) 234-3497

Joan DellaValle, Principal, Otsego Elementary School, 55 Otsego Street, Dix Hills, NY 11746. Phone: (516) 595-2760

Sherrye Dotson, District Curriculum Coordinator, Administration Building, Jacksonville Public Schools, Jacksonville, TX 75766. Phone: (903) 586-7208

Kenneth Dunn, Chair, Department of Administration and Supervision, School of Education, Queens College, CUNY, Main Street, Flushing, NY 11367-1597. Phone: (718) 997-5200

Larry Howie, Teacher, John A. McManus Elementary School, Chico Unified School District, 988 East Avenue, Chico, CA 95928-5999. Phone: (916) 891-3128

Penjiran Hajah Rahmah Pengiran Haji Jadid, 11, Villa Sejahtera, Simpang 528, Sungai Hanching, Julan Muara, Brunei Darussalam 3890

Bart Kelliher, Director of Special Education and Special Services, The Buffalo City Schools, 816 City Hall, Buffalo, NY 14202. Phone: (716) 851-3746

Angela Klavas, Assistant Director, Center for the Study of Learning and Teaching Styles, St. John's University, 8000 Utopia Parkway, Jamaica, NY 11439. Phone: (718) 990-6335 or (718) 990-6336
    An eight-day Learning Styles Leadership Certification Institute is held each July. For more information, contact the Center for the Study of Learning and Teaching Styles, St. John's University.

Paula Koshuta, Principal, Lowman Elementary School, Lowman, ID 83637

Mary Laffey, Principal, Oakland Junior High School, Columbia Public Schools, 3405 Oakland Place, Columbia, MO 65202. Phone: (314) 886-2710

Sister Natalie Lafser, Director, Office of Learning Styles, Saint Louis Archdiocese, 449 South Spring Avenue, St. Louis, MO 63116-4322. Phone: (314) 351-9097

Pat Lemmon, 3100 A Nutmeg Lane, Hutchinson, KS 67501. Phone: (316) 665-6333

Katy Lux and Connie Bouwman, Codirectors, North Central Learning Styles Center, Aquinas College, Grand Rapids, MI 48506. Phone: (616) 459-8281 or (800) 678-9593

Raja and Auvo Marckwort, MARCKWORT Training for Corporate Adults, Koulutusyhtiot, Korkeavuorenkatu 41 A 12, 00130 Helsinki, Finland. Phone: 607166. Fax: 358-0-611531

Jan Meritt, Science Teacher, Klammath Union High School, 1300 Montclaire Street, Klammath Falls, OR 97601. Phone: (503) 883-4714

Nancy Murphree, Mathematics Department Chair, Jacksonville Middle School, Jacksonville, TX 75766. Phone: (903) 586-7208

Denise Parker, Developmental Reading Teacher, Oakland Junior High School, Columbia Public Schools, 3405 Oakland Place, Columbia, MO 65202. Phone: (314) 886-2710

Janet Perrin, Principal, T.J. Lahey Elementary School, Pulaski Road, Greenlawn, NY 11740. Phone: (516) 754-5400

Jody Sands Taylor, Adjunct Professor, University of Virginia, 1008 West Franklin Street, Richmond, VA 23220. Phone: (804) 355-2033 or (804) 872-5411

Donald Treffinger, Director, Florida Learning Styles Center, Center for Creative Learning Inc., 4152 Independence Court, Suite C-7, Sarasota, FL 34234. Phone: (813) 351-8862

Sue Wellman, Science Teacher, Elm Lawn Elementary School, Middleton-Cross Plains Area Schools, 6701 Woodgate Road, Middleton, WI 53562. Phone: (608) 828-1660

Mary E. White, Mathematics Teacher, Oak Martin Middle School, 5650 Cahaba Valley Road, Birmingham, AL 35242. Phone: (205) 980-3660

Regina White, Principal, Bulkely Middle School, Box 351, Rhinebeck, NY 12572. Phone: (914) 871-5550

Media

Curry, L. (1987). *Integrating Concepts of Cognitive or Learning Styles: A Review with Attention to Psychometric Standards.* Ottawa: Ontario: Canadian College of Health Services Executives.

Dunn, R. (1994). *Examining Your Own Ethnocentric Beliefs in Light of Research Concerning the Learning Styles of Adolescents in Diverse Cultures* (audiotape). Alexandria, Va.: Association for Supervision and Curriculum Development.

Dunn, R. (1994). *Teaching Multicultural Students Through Their Learning Style Strengths* (videotape). Austin: Texas State Department of Education. This six-hour videotape is for educators concerned about increasing the effectiveness of staff development.

Dunn, R. (1994). *Teaching Students to READ Through Their Individual Learning Styles* (videotape). Austin: Texas State Department of Education. This six-hour videotape is for educators concerned about children's reading achievement. It was used in Education 7399.

Dunn, R. (1995). *How Learning Style Changes Over Time: Differences Among Students by Age and Gender* (audiotape). Alexandria, Va.: Association for Supervision and Curriculum Development.

Dunn, R. (1995). *Research Concerning the Learning Styles of Diverse Ethnic Groups* (audiotape). Alexandria, Va.: Association for Supervision and Curriculum Development.

Dunn, R. (1995). *Strategies for Educating Diverse Learners.* Bloomington, Ind.: Phi Delta Kappa. Provides hands-on, practical directions for translating any K-12 curriculum into a variety of styles-responsive resources.

Dunn, R., and K. Dunn. (1992). *Teaching Elementary Students Through Their Individual Learning Styles.* Boston: Allyn & Bacon. Provides hands-on, practical directions for translating any elementary school curriculum into a variety of styles-responsive instructional resources and floor plans. Includes samples of every strategy recommended.

Dunn, R., K. Dunn (1992, 1995) *Teaching Style Inventory Disc Software Package* (software). Jamaica, N.Y.: St. John's University's Center for the Study of Learning and Teaching Styles.

Dunn, R., and K. Dunn. (1993). *Teaching Secondary Students Through Their Individual Learning Styles.* Boston: Allyn & Bacon. Provides hands-on, practical directions for translating any secondary school curriculum into a variety of styles-responsive instructional resources and floor plans. Includes samples of every strategy recommended.

Dunn, R., and K. Dunn. (1994). *Providing Staff Development Through Teachers' Learning Styles* (videotape). Jamaica, N.Y.: St. John's University's Center for the Study of Learning and Teaching Styles. Six-hour videotape for educators concerned about increasing the effectiveness of staff development.

Dunn, R., K. Dunn, and J. Perrin. (1994). *Teaching Young Children Through Their Individual Learning Styles.* Boston: Allyn & Bacon. Provides hands-on, practical directions for translating any K-2 curriculum into a variety of styles-responsive resources and floor plans. Includes samples of every strategy recommended.

Dunn, R., and S.A. Griggs. (1995). *Multiculturalism and Learning Style: Teaching and Counseling Adolescents.* Westport, Conn.: Praeger. Provides insight into multicultural students and how they learn.

Griggs, S.A. (1991). *Counseling Students Through Their Individual Learning Styles.* Ann Arbor: The University of Michigan. An excellent guide for counselors. Available from Center for the Study of Learning and Teaching Styles, St. John's University, Jamaica, N.Y.

Milgram, R.M., R. Dunn, and G.E. Price, eds. (1993). *Teaching and Counseling Gifted and Talented Adolescents: An International Learning Style Perspective.* Westport, Conn.: Praeger. Provides insight into multicultural students and how they learn.

St. John's University's Center for the Study of Learning and Teaching Styles. (1980) *Learning Styles: An Explanation for Parents* (film and tape). Jamaica, N.Y.: Author.

St. John's University's Center for the Study of Learning and Teaching Styles. (1992). *Homework Disc Software Package* (software). Jamaica, N.Y.: Author. For $90 per school, the software can be used to individualize homework and prescribe each student's best learning styles environment.

St. John's University's Center for the Study of Learning and Teaching Styles. (1995). *Annotated Bibliography.* Jamaica, N.Y.: Author. This is the most complete overview of research on learning styles.

St. John's University's Center for the Study of Learning and Teaching Styles. (1995). *Learning Styles Network Newsletter.* Jamaica, N.Y.: Author. The Center for the Study of Learning and Teaching Styles at St. John's University and the National Association of Secondary School Principals publish this newsletter three times a year (since 1980) to disseminate learning styles research, the implementation of successful programs, new instructional resources, and staff development opportunities. Please contact the center when you successfully implement a learning styles program.

St. John's University's Center for the Study of Learning and Teaching Styles. (1996). *Articles and Books: A Compilation of the Best Studies and Practitioners' Reports on the Effects of Learning Style Approaches.* Jamaica, N.Y.: Author.

References

Alberg, J., L. Cook, T. Fiore, M. Friend, and S. Sano. (1992). *Educational Approaches and Options for Integrating Students With Disabilities: A Decision Tool.* Triangle Park, N.C.: Research Triangle Institute.

Andrews, R.H. (July-September 1990). "The Development of a Learning Styles Program in a Low Socioeconomic, Underachieving North Carolina Elementary School." *Journal of Reading, Writing, and Learning Disabilities International* 6, 3: 307-314.

Beaty, S.A. (1986). "The Effect of Inservice Training on the Ability of Teachers to Observe Learning Styles of Students." (Doctoral dissertation, Oregon State University, 1986.) *Dissertation Abstracts International* 47, 1998A.

Bouwman, C. (1991). *A Guide to Explaining Learning Styles to High School Students.* Jamaica, N.Y.: St. John's University's Center for the Study of Learning and Teaching Styles.

Braio, A. (1988). *Mission from No-Style.* Jamaica, N.Y.: St. John's University's Center for the Study of Learning and Teaching Styles.

Braio, A. (1990). *Return to No-Style.* Jamaica, N.Y.: St. John's University's Center for the Study of Learning and Teaching Styles.

Brunner, C.E., and W.S. Majewski. (October 1990). "Mildly Handicapped Students Can Succeed with Learning Styles." *Educational Leadership* 48, 2: 21-23.

Clark-Thayer, S. (1987). "The Relationship of the Knowledge of Student-Perceived Learning Style Preferences, and Study Habits and Attitudes to Achievement of College Freshmen in a Small Urban University." (Doctoral dissertation, Boston University, 1987). *Dissertation Abstracts International* 48: 872A.

DeBello, T. (July-September 1990). "Comparison of Eleven Major Learning Styles Models: Variables, Appropriate Populations, Validity of Instrumentation, and the Research Behind Them." *Journal of Reading, Writing, and Learning Disabilities International* 6, 3: 203-222.

Dunn, R. (1987). "Research on Instructional Environments: Implications for Student Achievement and Attitudes." *Professional School Psychology* 2, 1: 43-52.

Dunn, R. (1988). "Commentary: Teaching Students Through Their Perceptual Strengths or Preferences." *Journal of Reading* 31, 4: 304-309.

Dunn, R. (1989). "Individualizing Instruction for Mainstreamed Gifted Children." In *Teaching Gifted and Talented Learners In Regular Classrooms*, edited by R.R. Milgram. Springfield, Ill.: Charles C. Thomas.

Dunn, R. (1995). *Strategies for Educating Diverse Learners.* Bloomington, Ind.: Phi Delta Kappa.

Dunn, R., J.S. Beaudry, and A. Klavas. (March 1989). "Survey of Research on Learning Styles." *Educational Leadership* 46, 6: 50-58.

Dunn, R., J. Bruno, R.I. Sklar, R. Zenhausern, and J. Beaudry. (May/June 1990). "Effects of Matching and Mismatching Minority Developmental College Students' Hemispheric Preferences on Mathematics Scores." *Journal of Educational Research* 83, 5: 283-288.

Dunn, R., D. Cavanaugh, B. Eberle, and R. Zenhausern. (1982). "Hemispheric Preference: The Newest Element of Learning Style." *The American Biology Teacher* 44, 5: 291-294.

Dunn, R., J. DellaValle, K. Dunn, G. Geisert, R. Sinatra, and R. Zenhausern. (1986). "The Effects of Matching and Mismatching Students' Mobility Preferences on Recognition and Memory Tasks." *Journal of Educational Research* 79, 5: 267-272.

Dunn, R., and K. Dunn. (1972). *Practical Approaches to Individualizing Instruction: Contracts and Other Effective Teaching Strategies.* Englewood Cliffs, N.J.: Prentice-Hall.

Dunn, R., and K. Dunn. (1992). *Teaching Elementary Students Through Their Individual Learning Styles.* Boston: Allyn & Bacon.

Dunn, R., and K. Dunn (producers and presenters). (1992, 1995). *Teaching Style Inventory Disc Software Package* (software). Jamaica, N.Y.: St. John's University's Center for the Study of Learning and Teaching Styles.

Dunn, R., and K. Dunn. (1993). *Teaching Secondary Students Through Their Individual Learning Styles.* Boston: Allyn & Bacon.

Dunn, R., K. Dunn, and J. Perrin. (1994). *Teaching Young Children Through Their Individual Learning Styles.* Boston: Allyn & Bacon.

Dunn, R., K. Dunn, and G.E. Price. (1974, 1978, 1984, 1989). *Learning Style Inventory.* Available from Price Systems, Box 1818-66044, Lawrence, KS 66044. The *LSI* is available on IBM and Macintosh self-scoring disks.

Dunn, R., K. Dunn, and G.E. Price. (1977). "Diagnosing Learning Styles: Avoiding Malpractice Suits Against School Systems." *Phi Delta Kappan* 58, 5: 418-420.

Dunn, R., K. Dunn, and G.E. Price. (1989). *Productivity Environmental Preference Survey.* Available from Price Systems, Box 1818-66044, Lawrence, Kan. 66044.

Dunn, R., K. Dunn, L. Primavera, R. Sinatra, and J. Virostko. (1987). "A Timely Solution: A Review of Research on the Effects of Chronobiology on Children's Achievement and Behavior." *The Clearing House* 61, 1: 5-8.

Dunn, R., K. Dunn, and D. Treffinger. (1992). *Bringing out the Giftedness in Every Child: A Guide for Parents.* New York: John Wiley and Sons.

Dunn, R., M.C. Giannitti, J.B. Murray, G. Geisert, I. Rossi, and P. Quinn. (August 1990). "Grouping Students for Instruction: Effects of Individual vs. Group Learning Style on Achievement and Attitudes." *Journal of Social Psychology* 130, 4: 485-494.

Dunn, R., and S. Griggs. (1988). *Learning Styles: Quiet Revolution in American Secondary Schools.* Reston, Va.: National Association of Secondary School Principals.

Dunn, R., and S.A. Griggs. (1990). "Research on the Learning Style Characteristics of Selected Racial and Ethnic Groups." *Journal of Reading, Writing, and Learning Disabilities* 6, 3: 261-280.

Dunn, R., and S.A. Griggs. (1995). *Multiculturalism and Learning Style: Teaching and Counseling Adolescents.* Westport, Conn.: Praeger.

Dunn, R., S.A. Griggs, J. Olson, B. Gorman, and M. Beasley. (1995). "A Meta Analytic Validation of the Dunn and Dunn Learning Styles Model." *Journal of Educational Research*, 88, 6: 353-361.

Dunn, R. and A. Klavas. (1992a). *Homework Disc Software Package* (software). Jamaica, N.Y.: St. John's University's Center for the Study of Learning and Teaching Styles.

Dunn, R., and A. Klavas. (1992b). *Interpreting Adults' Productivity Style Software Package* (software). Jamaica, N.Y.: St. John's University's Center for the Study of Learning and Teaching Styles.

Dunn, R., J. Krimsky, J. Murray, and P. Quinn. (1985). Light up Their Lives: A Review of Research on the Effects of Lighting on Children's Achievement." *The Reading Teacher* 38, 9: 863-869.

Elliot, I. (November/December 1991). "The Reading Place." *Teaching K-8* 21, 3: 30-34.

Gadwa, K., and S.A. Griggs. (1985). "The School Dropout: Implications for Counselors." *The School Counselor* 33: 9-17.

Griggs, D., S.A. Griggs, R. Dunn, and J. Ingham. (1994). "A Challenge for Nurse Educators: Accommodating Nursing Students' Diverse Learning Styles." *Nurse Educator* 19, 6: 41-45.

Harp, T.Y., and L. Orsak. (July-September 1990). "One Administrator's Challenge: Implementing a Learning Style Program at the Secondary Level." *Journal of Reading, Writing, and Learning Disabilities International* 6, 3: 335-342.

Hill, J.S. (1976). *Cognitive Style Interest Inventory.* Available from Oakland Community College, 2480 Opdyke Road, Bloomfield Hills, Mich. 48013.

Hodges, H. (1985). "An Analysis of the Relationships Among Preferences for a Formal/Informal Design, One Element of Learning Style, Academic Achievement, and Attitudes of Seventh and Eighth Grade Students in Remedial Mathematics Classes in a New York City Junior High School." (Doctoral dissertation, St. John's University, 1985.) *Dissertation Abstracts International* 45: 2791A.

Keefe, J.W., M. Languis, C. Letteri, and R. Dunn (1986). *NASSP Learning Style Profile.* Reston, Va.: National Association of Secondary School Principals.

Kirby, P. (1979). *Cognitive Style, Learning Style, and Transfer Skill Acquisition.* Columbus: The Ohio State University, National Center for Research in Vocational Education.

Klavas, A. (1993). "In Greensboro, North Carolina: Learning Style Program Boosts Achievement and Test Scores." *The Clearing House* 67, 3: 149-151.

Klavas, A., R. Dunn, S.A. Griggs, J. Gemake, G. Geisert, and R. Zenhausern. (1994). "Factors that Facilitated or Impeded Implementation of the Dunn and Dunn Learning Style Model." *Illinois School Research and Development Journal* 31, 1: 19-23.

Koshuta, V., and P. Koshuta. (April 1993). "Learning Styles in a One-Room School." *Educational Leadership* 50, 7: 87.

Kyriacou, M., and R. Dunn. (1994). "Synthesis of Research: Learning Styles of Students with Learning Disabilities." *Special Education Journal* 4, 1: 3-9.

Lemmon, P. (1985). "A School Where Learning Styles Make a Difference." *Principal* 64, 4: 26-29.

Lenehan, M.C. (1991). *Kids in Style.* Jamaica, N.Y.: St. John's University's Center for the Study of Learning and Teaching Styles.

Lenehan, M.C., R. Dunn., J. Ingham, W. Murray, and B. Signer. (1994). "Learning Style: Necessary Know-How for Academic Success in College." *Journal of College Student Development* 35, 461-465.

Levy, J., and P. Riordan. (1995). "How Important are Rank-in-Class and Grade-Point Average to College Admissions?" *Inter-Ed.* 23 (75), 15-18.

Marcus, L. (1977). "How Teachers View Learning Styles." *NASSP Bulletin* 61, 408: 112-114.

Mickler, M.L., and C.P. Zippert. (1987). "Teaching Strategies Based on Learning Styles of Adult Students." *Community/Junior College Quarterly* 11: 33-37.

Milgram, R.M., R. Dunn, and G.E. Price, eds. (1993). *Teaching and Counseling Gifted and Talented Adolescents: An International Learning Style Perspective.* Westport, Conn.: Praeger.

Neely, R.O., and D. Alm. (1992). "Meeting Individual Needs: A Learning Styles Success Story." *The Clearing House* 2, 109-113.

Neely, R.O., and D. Alm. (1993). "Empowering Students with Styles." *Principal* 72, 4: 32-35.

Nelson, B., R. Dunn, S.A. Griggs, L. Primavera, M. Fitzpatrick. (1993). "Effects of Learning Style Intervention on Students' Retention and Achievement." *Journal of College Student Development* 34, 5: 364-369.

Nganwa-Bagumah, M. (1986). "Learning Styles: The Effects of Matching and Mismatching Pupils' Design Preferences on Reading Comprehension Tests." (Bachelor's diss., University of Transkei, South Africa.)

Nganwa-Bagumah, M., and T.S. Mwamwenda. (1991). "Effects on Reading Comprehension Tests of Matching and Mismatching Student's Design Preferences." *Perceptual and Motor Skills* 72, 3: 947-951.

Orsak, L. (1990a). "Learning Styles and Love: A Winning Combination." *Journal of Reading, Writing, and Learning Disabilities: International* 6, 3: 343-347.

Orsak, L. (October 1990b). "Learning Styles Versus the Rip Van Winkle Syndrome." *Educational Leadership* 48, 2: 19-21.

Ott, J.N. (1973). *Health and Light: The Effects of Natural Light and Artificial Light on Man and Other Living Things.* Old Greenwich, Conn.: The Devin-Adair Co.

Pena, R. (1989). *Two-of-a-Kind Learning Styles.* Jamaica, N.Y.: St. John's University's Center for the Study of Learning and Teaching Styles.

Perrin, J. (1982). *Learning Style Inventory: Primary Version.* Jamaica, N.Y.: St. John's University's Center for the Study of Learning and Teaching Styles.

Perrin, J. (1984). "An Experimental Investigation of the Relationships Among the Learning Style Sociological Preferences of Gifted and Non-Gifted Primary Children, Selected Instructional Strategies, Attitudes, and Achievement in Problem Solving and Rote Memorization." (Doctoral diss., St. John's University). *Dissertation Abstracts International* 46: 342A.

Perrin, J. (October 1990). "The Learning Styles Project for Potential Dropouts." *Educational Leadership* 48, 2: 23-24.

Perrin, J., and S. Santora. (1982). *Elephant Style.* Jamaica, N.Y.: St. John's University's Center for the Study of Learning and Teaching Styles.

Pizzo, J., R. Dunn, and K. Dunn. (July/September 1990). "A Sound Approach to Reading: Responding to Students' Learning Styles." *Journal of Reading, Writing, and Learning Disabilities International* 6, 3: 249-260.

Quinn, R. (1993). "The New York State Compact for Learning and Learning Styles." *Learning Styles Network Newsletter* 15, 1: 1-2.

Restak, R. (1979). *The Brain: The Last Frontier.* New York: Doubleday.

St. John's University's Center for the Study of Learning and Teaching Styles. (1996). *Research on the Dunn and Dunn Model.* Jamaica, N.Y.: Author.

Shea, T.C. (1983). "An Investigation of the Relationship Among Preferences for the Learning Style Element of Design, Selected Instructional Environments, and Reading Achievement with Ninth Grade Students to Improve Administrative Determinations Concerning Effective Educational Facilities." (Doctoral diss., St. John's University). *Dissertation Abstracts International* 44: 2004A.

Stone, P. (November 1992). "How We Turned Around a Problem School." *The Principal* 71, 2: 34-36.

Studd, M. (1995). "Learning-Style Differences." *The Clearing House* 69, 1: 38-39.

Thies, A.P. (1979). "A Brain Behavior Analysis of Learning Style." In *Student Learning Styles: Diagnosing and Prescribing Programs.* Reston, Va.: National Association of Secondary School Principals.

Turner, N.D. (Summer 1993). "Learning Styles and Metacognition." *Reading Improvement* 30, 2: 82-85.

446093